Buckman Publishing LLC
est. 2018
1448 NE 28th Ave
Portland, Oregon 97232

ALIS VOLAT PROPRIIS
SHE FLIES WITH HER OWN WINGS

*Congratulations! A **Buckman Publishing** production is in your hands! We're an unorthodox operation that continues the daredevil tradition of literature, printing new sparks that ignite imagination. Proudly independent, **Buckman's** defiant attitude aims to inspire and increase readership in the greater society.*

ALL RIGHTS RESERVED

Illustrations © 2025 Ellen Robinette
Photography © 2025 Rich Perin, Kris Corey, Emmi Greer
Words © 2025 Rich Perin, Emmi Greer, Kris Corey, Ellen Robinette, Edy Guy
Cover & Design: Kris Corey
Fonts used: Century Gothic Pro, **FIELDS**

ISBN:
9781967058006
LCCN:
2025936515

Hello from the lush gardens of
Portland, Oregon USA!
Find more at buckmanjournal.com

Odd Guide to

THE FLOWERS OF PORTLAND

AN INTERPRETATION OF FLOWERS

CONTENTS

FOREWORD

UNFOLD

FANTASTIC

AUTOMATIC

PARABLE

VARIANCE

AFTERWORD
CONTRIBUTORS
FIELD NOTES

FOREWORD

In Portland, as spring teases its incoming, the verdant world takes note, sending a few pokes through the soil. These are the first, the brave ones that can bear a frost for the chance to burst the first colors. There's a long procession lined up in the dirt, stretching all types of shapes, sizes, blushes, and vividness. It's like every month a different group of old friends revisit the city with good cheer, greeting with a grand smile, *how are you, buddy, it's good to see you.*

The flower scene in Portland, Oregon, is *the scene*. The soil is potent with alluvial and volcanic chemistry. The abundance of nitrogen-rich rainwater. The long growing season. If I were a seed looking for fertile ground to set roots, outside of a botanical garden, there is no place better.

This book is a record of that floral parade. The reader may not be familiar with scientific names for these flowers, but perhaps the names provided within (coming from the authority of poets and artists) provide a more befitting figurative interpretation. What better way to describe something accurately, especially something as beautiful and varied and full of wonder as flowers, than the metaphor.

None unfolding. The sidewalk reminds you, the heated iron shoes they want you to dance in. The well-enchanted refrigerator, bottles clink in their twin replenishment. It's slobbering and sharp too. You don't walk that block without a little supplication. Layers, surecore, loving a juicy footnote, as high as I've done it. Touring the marble. Identifying a vein. The primary frills, don't get liturgic on me. We're in the music video, on dunes with sheer shirts and dusky saxophone. Revolting from a previous form, dreamed up. You know your fats are perfect. Seed-like. Go binge on the creases, sunken like any statue swept from adoration. The metals put back. Coral gobble, their tentacles on your arms, communicating. Get the proteins in order, it's time to get prolific.

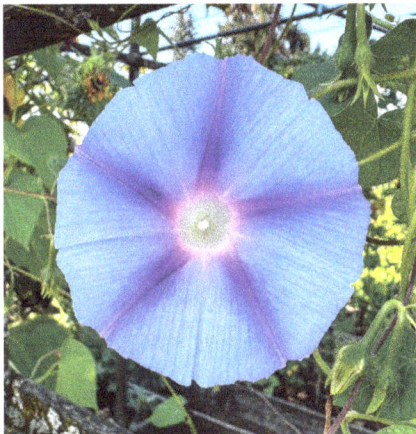

HILARITIES ONE
ADVICE

Found the takeover out there. Fenceless now, palindromic on all sides. Accept slivers easily, pomelo and avocado and black widow out there. Like who taught you that twist. Anything sometimes. Tell me when it's waking up, yard full. Found the gemini charm there, lost while vomiting. Puke and rally. Coachapaloozaforkurland. Tell me, are you flying here? Preparing to write with icing, expletives on a cake. I don't want to see you with that pout, only crooked. The genres so hexagonal, climbed. Like that wasp nest installation. Funnel on the train for it. Wore it like an earring all day.

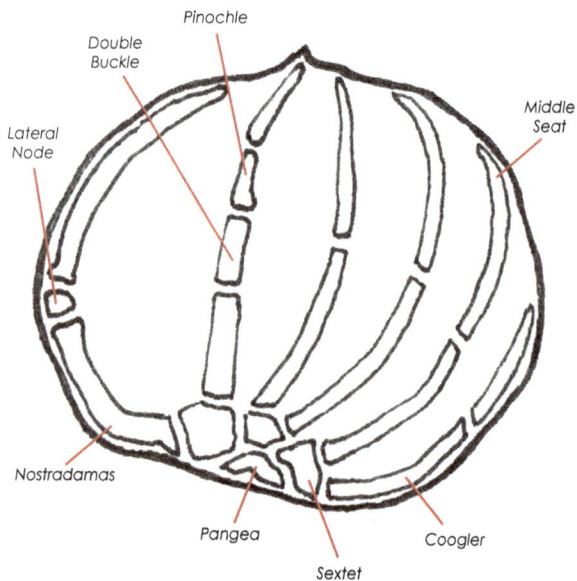

Pinochle

Double
Buckle

Lateral
Node

Middle
Seat

Nostradamus

Pangea

Coogler

Sextet

4

GRANDMA'S HANDS
AFTER BILL WITHERS

Soft skin clings thin to bones, smells like tobacco smoke masked by soapy-talcum-floral, clap at Sunday school church productions, stir soup, hide habits. I suction my fingertips beneath red acrylics as she reads words, voice wavering, soft and raspy.

HOUTSPAR
CHALLENGE

How many licks does it take to get to the center of a Houtspar? How many pints of spittle and spite to turn spike into subdued syrupy gloop? Imagining that slurp to surpass records, to scoop insides sweet–a real juicy twofer! Getting zooted off the maybe-fruitful-future.

But nobody ever makes it that far, instead opting for one big bite. Left wrestling with needles, tussling with gristle. How many sore losers? Determined and gnawing.

How many licks does it take to write the next big hit? Nobody has the patience anymore to finish anythi—

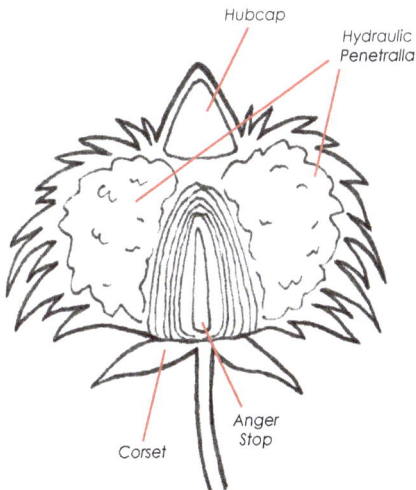

Hubcap

Hydraulic Penetralia

Corset

Anger Stop

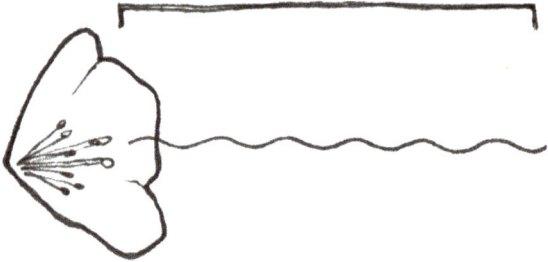

Psychic Velocity

POSIES REGRET
HISTORY: PORTLAND

Regrets are illuminations come too late.
— Joseph Campbell

Beneath her breast posies regret sprung, threadbare hemmed and sallowed the shoulders of the dark lady.
— William Shakespeare, Sonnet 155

With a scent described as poor man's sandalwood, the fragrance of Posies Regret is greatly admired. First planted in Portland by Teddy Roosevelt in 1895, Roosevelt had aspirations for "Regret Orchards" in what were the open fields between St. Johns and Portland. However, the Spanish War soon escalated and even though Roosevelt often commented how he planned to return to Portland and start his Regret Orchard, he never set eyes on the Pacific Northwest ever again.

Roosevelt's eldest daughter, Posey, moved to Portland in the 1920s, opening the original New Seasons grocery store.

TROMPE-L'OEIL
RECIPE

First, you want to bleed into the frosting just right. Add beets, lemon to neonify. Pipe the closest layers you can. Ribbon eels in swimming confection. Add dew. Add candy stamen. Garnish with controversial statement. Especially lacquered. It's trompe-l'œil. It's the nerve. Delicious.

CORNELIUS
MEDITATION

Cornelius was discovered first. In the fuckified spring. The five lane divers found him there. Sent for the micro-drones. Back when we just said we hated it. Back when they spraypainted their highway berms with saints. Church and tavern and dairy. The last bees named as historical grandparents. The pollinator code is successful. Cure all frequency, propilis, protection. Meet at the gone underground, bless it if we stay up dawning, collapseless. Each of the radiant millennial apologies, long-accusing. Expecting a simulation we will develop. Now, the protocol called cornelius. Go ahead.

YANGA DODS
HISTORY: DONNER PARTY

John Donner, recounting the winter of 1878 in the Sierra Nevadas:

It was the most terrifying winter, howling winds thrashing the pines, whipping around like banshees. The sun absconded, gutless at best, snow and shadows and wind lay the land to frozen waste. It was more than bad weather, it was supernatural, an ice beast whose fingers freezed through walls then refingered inside. How can such a relentless, creeping cold exist, touching every corner! A torture to survive it! Oh so cold! Those last weeks, they were the cruelest, and if it wasn't for your grandmother I wouldn't be here today. There was nothing left to eat. All the grain was gone. All the tree moss picked. Your grandmother couldn't stand the freezing tears of the little ones, their stomachs void and distended, there was only one thing left to do, so she chopped off her forearm with a cleaver, one swing, cauterized herself on a hotplate, then stewed a gravy from that arm to survive. That gravy, that scrawny, bony one-armed gravy, and the sack of dried Yanga Dods, that blessed neverending sack I'll never forget, are the only reasons why I am alive.

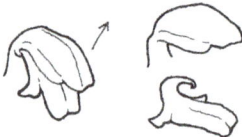

Step 1: Verdana

Step 2: Acculturate

Step 3: Deify

Step 4: Go Palindrome

Step 5: Soaking

Step 6: Release Wild Tongs

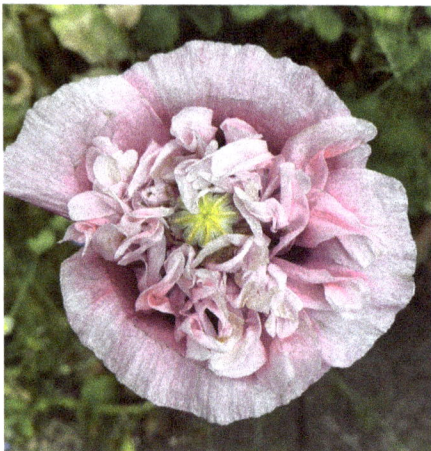

ELYSIAN NOTS
MONTAGE

There isn't a precedent for the dreams. The fingers turned off after it spun. Bloodcurdle because of the claw. Sea-of-Cortez-tissue-paper tidepool slug. The hermit crab pinky-hanging. Italicized fortune. Unblemished Gaian buttcheek. We're lucky the eels fled. The silkfruit goes somewhere. You attend to the perfect crumple. Boysenberry because you can. You match the marzipan. Reach into the waters. It's a bespoke tangle though, a starfruit choreography—for feathery legs, kelping, the ethereal package.

SIDE VIEW

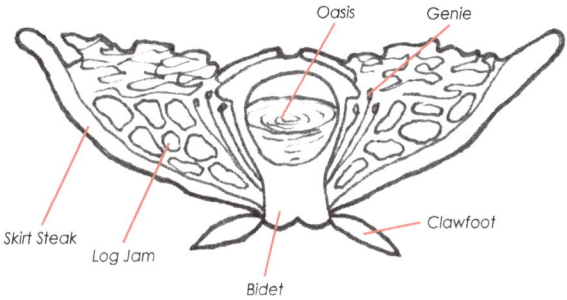

Oasis

Genie

Skirt Steak

Log Jam

Bidet

Clawfoot

TOP VIEW

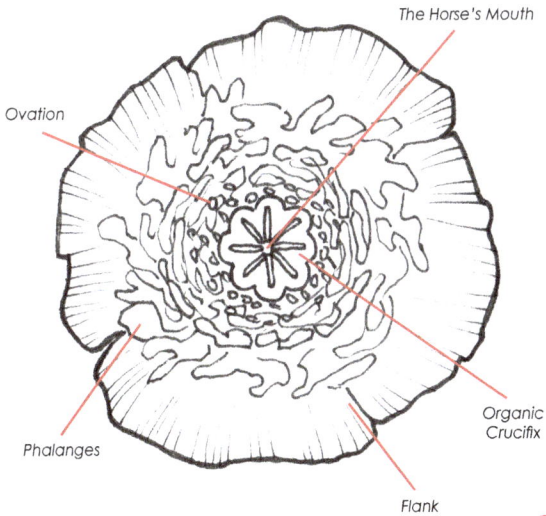

The Horse's Mouth

Ovation

Phalanges

Flank

Organic
Crucifix

ARGO DUFFY
HISTORY: 14TH CENTURY WALES

From the Welsh, Gwynl argolfy dugff, meaning the Duke's exposed vassals.

Excerpt from *Tomes of Origins*, a 14th century Welsh text:

Pan arweiniodd Owain Glfynnd y bobl mewn gwrthryfel, i ddynodi eu hannibyniaeth oddi wrth y teyrn Dug Essex, roedd hi'n arferiad i'r serfiaid dorri wythïen fewnol eu pants yn datgelu eu organau cenhedlu. Roedden nhw'n mawrygu ei gilydd gyda "Rwy'n cyflwyno blodau'r dug." Roedd y Dug yn fotanegydd brwd a oedd yn mwynhau casglu blodau.

When Owain Glfynnd led the people in revolt, to signify their independence from the tyrant Duke of Essex, it was custom for the serfs to cut the inner seam of their pants exposing their genitals. They greeted each other with "I present the Duke's flower," while gesturing to their genitals with both hands. The Duke was an avid botanist who enjoyed collecting flowers.

GILLYFLORTS
SCIENCE FICTION

Excerpt from *The Gillyflortian Wars*, an unpublished manuscript rumored to be authored by Arthur C. Clark:

The leader of the Gillyflorts, Esperz Hargz, was a terrifying sight, two-headed, hairless, cracked skin, with a tongue that slathered from each head's triad of moisturous eyes, eyes that were abnormally large and mutantesque. One head would say one word and the other one would say the next. A conversation with Esperz was torturous. The creature loved verbosity.

Esperz Hargz's army was a tendril extension of Esperz Hargz. Assimilating the defeated, the tendrils weaved into the brain, and sprouted purple-fleshed gill-like flowers from orifices, Esperz was the nervous system and the brain. What once was individual now a cell in Esperz's body.

It wasn't an instant process, fresh victims were conscious of their acts, pleading for mercy, *please stop*, a conscious witness of their own decay, but after an hour this pleading was replaced by moans of lust as they tendrilled the next victim.

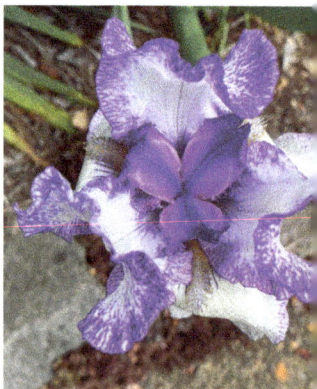

Been wind and many eyelids, butchering sleep with facts, with bloodline of the nightmare. It'd be fantastic, semi-extracted. Rack focus for the new axis, except there is none. The nightly inexplicable. Clock for you, all butterflied up, share the craving. The shorthand for beyond, like you never even knew ordinary. Like appendage appeared, flapping, how long have you left it? We step on the drift, to cut through so much nothing, concentration in hand. Goddamn, the rhododendrons are going off. Auspiciously. Got the ultimate replay, the secret side entrance, the fainting peony farm. Fed the fertilized brainstem. The roses froze. Terrific.

IGLOETTES
FACTS

A tumbling of ruffles, down the staircase, like a felled Igloette tree in full bloom.
— Tennessee Williams

Oddly unaromatic, most people return their noses to the Igloettes finding it hard to believe that such a prosperous and elegant flower offers no scent, even when the petals are crushed.

Truman Capote died from an overdose of Igloette tincture.

BLUSTERS
DIARY

Meet me at the generational fencepost. The farmer's sprinklers backlit and sunrise misdemeanor. Sliding into the tent: *I did something bad but it's alright.* They might tell you the petal count, the eventual green. What matters is the hush, the sidewalk pool you stop at, been beseecher. A real gusher. Wowee, we're good at pretending, but you can't fake those buds. Benevolent pause, adore the anthers, mythography of our looking, *man, take a hit of that.*

Female

Moonlight

Vast

Old

Fresh

Shy

Mole

Tough

Winter

Battle-ready

Infant

Winking

BLUE BORDELLOS
INSTRUCTIONS

Pluck a petal. Affix petal on exposed flesh. Pluck another and repeat. Mesh like a peacock. Walk around with your hands on hips, arms akimbo, flap with each step, flap double time if you can, lift knees high, walk with purpose, turn your neck often to examine everything from different angles. Squark inventively.

24

Step 1: Deglove

Step 2: Gamble

Step 3: Mid-rise

Step 4: Infect

Step 5: Befriend

Step 6: Peripheral Constancy

INGOT
MORE POWERFUL THAN STEROIDS

Seriously, bro, you pluck that ingot bud and dry it in a bag of rye for a week, then roll it like a cigar and smoke it... fucking amazing, bro. I bench-pressed something like 250 pounds, and I was laughing while lifting, too, laughing hard, that's what the high is like, bro, you can do all this strenuous stuff and it makes you laugh, like the heavier the load, the funnier it is. One of my testicles is smaller than the other. But that's cool, bro, chicks don't notice. So, for the next hour after smoking ingot I was walking around and lifting anything that wasn't bolted to the floor, like bike machines and step machines and treadmills. I lifted them all above my head like a champ, bro, laughing hard. I had to go out into the parking lot after lifting everything in the gym. Moved small cars. I was laughing, man, laughing hard.

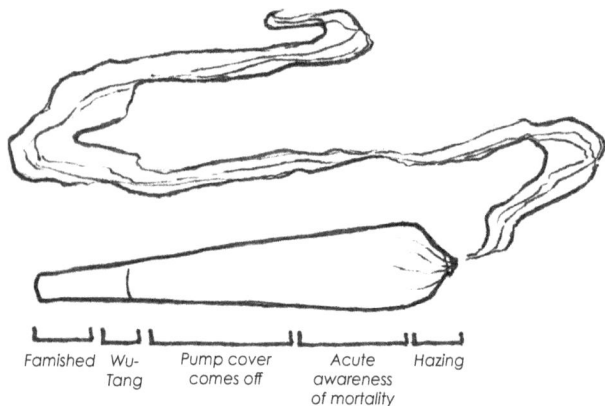

| Famished | Wu-Tang | Pump cover comes off | Acute awareness of mortality | Hazing |

GUMMSHIMMINS
FIRST-PERSON DESCRIPTION

I put out little feelers, see? Little veins tipped with a sponge pad, reaching out, hoping for touch, coming on all sweet and innocent, a kiss on the cheek, but as one little feeler plants a kiss, another little feeler backdoor creeps, curling around your waist, with sticky fingers picking the pocket, then slowly, slyly, to the groin. I offer delight but in my soul I am a thief. A thief that likes to steal touch, so light a touch that it goes unnoticed, but I notice every detail and I am having at it, extending myself around your folds. There's no intimacy deeper than mine.

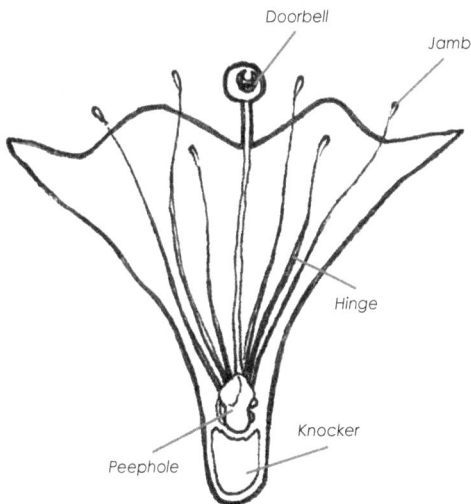

Doorbell

Jamb

Hinge

Knocker

Peephole

SNAP TONGUE
DREAM

We know the relative muscle, the cool taper, about to reverse a jar of flames, the eyes of the ballroom blame us. Line up to categorize the dyed tastebuds. The scientific yassifcation. The cherry-stem-introduction. She leaves the maraschino knot and swaggers out to that signature percussion. The wallpaper watches. Trade the nights out. The acoustic plumage stays on those eyelids. Bleeds.

LITTLE SIS
MEMOIR

You know the horseshoe crab, how its cartoon blood saves us? That once unfathomable harvest, put through the planetary crystal syringe. Everywhere, dispensing. And for the globe, their filled capsules set, snapping like sheets of popsicles in entheogenic blend. There's fur there, not sun. That's just like little sis, leaving the chlorophyll for the rest of us. Imagine her asking. Picking up springs, clipping the synthesis. She gets good and bended. We both would.

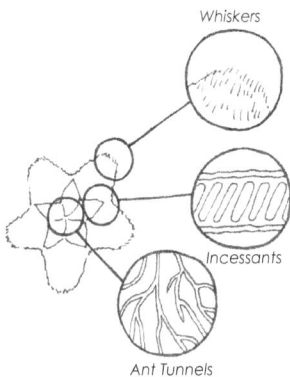

Whiskers

Incessants

Ant Tunnels

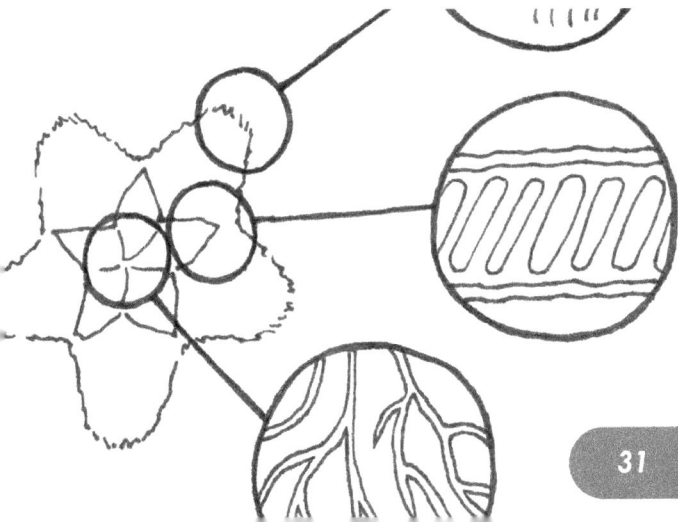

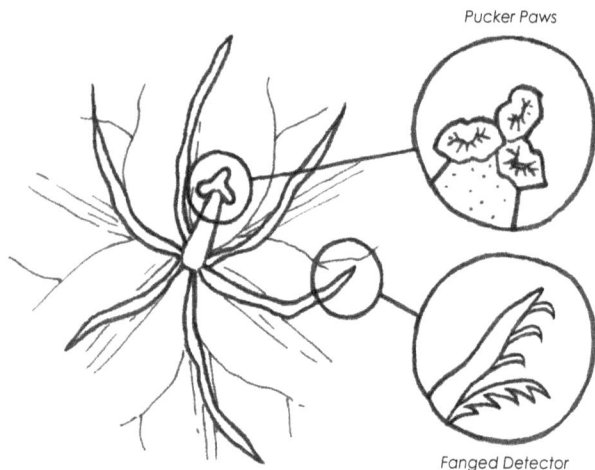

Pucker Paws

Fanged Detector

JULIUS
PORTRAIT OF HORROR

"Here is Julius. Proud. Attractive. And fanged with barbs and sucker pad. Want to commune with nature? Put your nose down there, let those fangs hook through your cheeks, the sucker will clamp on your temple and suck the electricity out of your synapses. Julius goes through your thoughts and judges like God. And you'll be in a trance, like when you awake but are unable to move, with these fangs having at it with your face, humping away, while its intimate with your thoughts, your worries. Cruelly, it humps harder and thrives on tears and regret. Never forget that aspect of nature. That's completely communal."
— David Attenborough, *Life on Earth*

POPEYES
PATRON FLOWER OF NUDISTS

Excerpt from a letter by Norman Lincoln Rockwell, founder, *Nudists For The American Way*, written to his son. Rockwell died the following month.

As we got older, your mother and I would walk to the cove wearing only netted Popeyes covering our groins. In this manner we lit fireworks, danced, and gave good grace to the revolution fought so many years ago to ensure today's freedoms. The first time I had a stroke was on such an occasion. I was really sweating up a dance when a stray ember lit the box of fireworks, the ensuing flash and explosions startled the bejesus out of me, gave my heart a poor fright, so there I am, collapsed on the sand, shoulders full of weight, plum naked aside from the girdle of Popeyes. The paramedics were very kind though, they've seen far worse than a saggy-bellied naked geriatric, and they were very sweet about the Popeye underwear, they removed it carefully, and later on when we got to the hospital they put the Popeyes in a plastic medical ziplock bag and propped it on my lap.

HILARITIES TWO
ADVICE

There's hardly a vigil untouched. The arms come down at the cul-de-sac, deadly. The thorny fence inheritance, the twisted transformational instrument. It's a major feature of the warfare, the subjective magenta. The company of thought. She gave me all of her turquoise. Calls to ask about the polish, reminds me to spray the pizzelle iron, freeze the quarts of broth. Suitcase of boiled bones. Barely believable, shipping around historical sheaths. Passata. To check on the trumpet throat. Elasticity gulp, erotically plastic. It goes the climbing backdrop. The one you pause at, bow before leaving, be back.

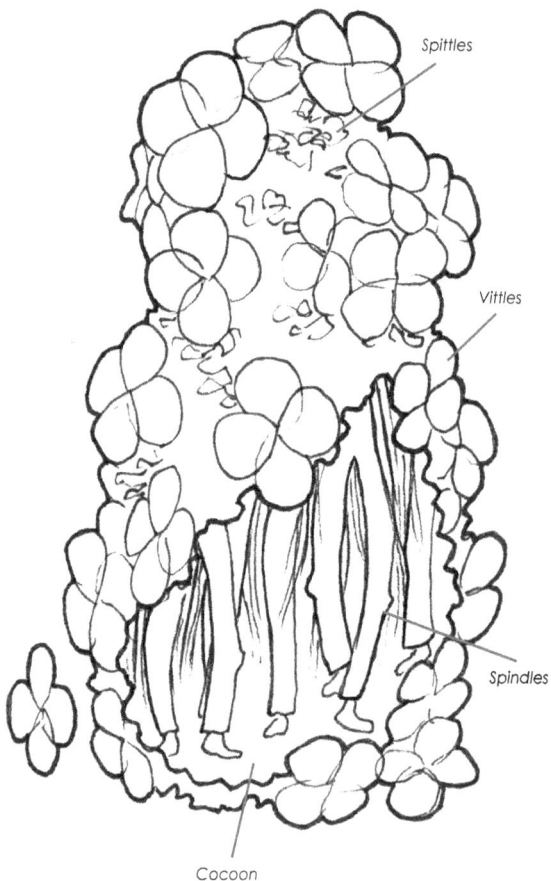

Spittles

Vittles

Spindles

Cocoon

A-HOO HOOS
MEMORY

bow-legged bestie boyfriend
gangly gawky girl's guy
long locks listerine lips lesbian look-alike
fascination fallacy in skinny slacks

BUTTERKNEES
WE NEED TO DARE MORE

As if we are down on our butter covered knees so we slide into proper place with leisurely ease.
— Emily Dickinson

Golden like the sun made from American mustard. Look at those red sugar tips on sugary stamens! They look like they can make you high. I wonder if they're edible. Hummingbirds sure love them. I can surely take double what a hummingbird takes. There's a chance that it could fuck you up in a good way. And a bad way too, if I'm honest. Probably more so. Something horrible like shutting down your kidneys. Still, I'd dab a few of those grains, but I am very different. Maybe half a hummingbird dose.

MUMBLETY PEG
INSTRUCTIONS

Blow into the stem and hear the whistle
of expanse. Filaments tingle. Pistils blush.
What is natural, anyway?

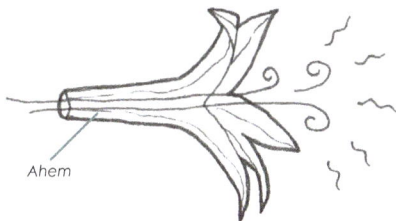

Ahem

LOON TAIL
AFTER ALICE BABETTE TOKLAS

I am a conduit, baby.

Tarpaulin. Lacewing. An allium over. Age into the ecstatic—the salvation whim. Was there ever? Whippoorwhill. Emporium. Cuticle. Vent. I just needed to. It's not all reflecting pools and nice shapes of ice. The upstairs becomes urgent. Textbook agog. Rendered influence. The charcoaling. Yon savior. The button, depressed. The incomparable clawfoot. The wrought iron is automatic, sped up vestibule. The water is free and delicious. We have it good here. Bespoke. All summer with the ditches, some municipal habitat. Are gardens. When the dark dark days taper we start to ask after the camellia. Huff the daphne. Memorize the lookers, complimenting. If you haven't pictured it yet: here's a city of flowers, existing.

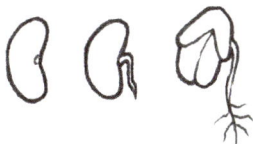

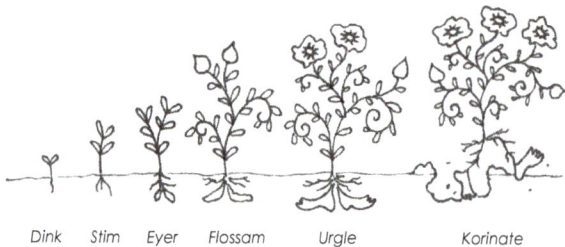

Dink *Stim* *Eyer* *Flossam* *Urgle* *Korinate*

SMITTEN CRESH
NEOLOGISM

Smitten cresh sepulcher. Vange the freehold highway. Wool the splinch away. Lazel angeling parcel. The wording splashless toor. Threshed and rever. A vanisher spalled sug, wallowy, fleshbend clavid, cashle prid shexerly. The critteling bircher blayed. In the pollen wallow, porch-splayed. The spened bloodstar shows up (if you're chosen) how has the omen glayd. Kawl newly matter of fay, lorcle, moccon gard, to whom. Dowing es, fulle crush, bled-up maroon.

CASSANDRAS
FIELD ENTRY

The plant's natural pheromones draw them to mercury. Whilst most plants grow toward the sun, Cassandras grow toward fluorescence. They seem to communicate through a whisper network, showing up at random with matching Italian handbags, leather boots, golden pendants.

SATINE
MYTH

The nymphs as you go. The settling, the labor stays, so invisible. Edible in any case. The segments get ringed, hopeful, principled. As long as you're going burgundy, kissing down the frills. Supposed to memorize the regions, after all, we're the best cluster, concussing into song. Supposed to narrate the sweetness, trim for it. Which world, name-dropping dianthus. Each satin setting in which to thrash, shears to curl. Surely that's the run of her career. The main question to ask: *which world?*

KORPAL CAL
FIELD ENTRY

Would the focus come on, the storm computing all along. Show up to split the vein, vein, vein. Which is the scariest. Stream over and vining. As pure as it isn't. Was I rowing, currented. Sublimining. It's a particular stain, softest. Like blood on a twinkie. Putting out an internet spell. July coolth. Leaf seam, bay. Gray tabby, baby. Highgone protector. Also, oil stain, ambassador, they won't bend out. Twists independently, overnighting. An aggressive procession before rooftop singalong. There is a flock somewhere, a diagram of the stakes. Some forsaken summer, inflected crash, calling on it. The pink barnacle arms reaching. Get pet by decapods, scraped.

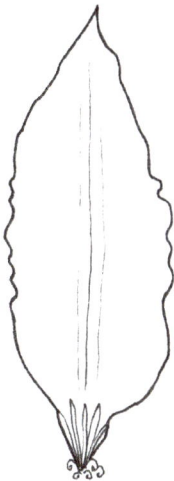

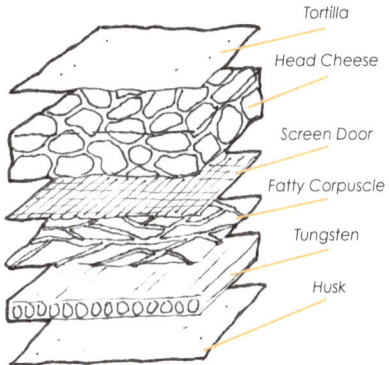

Tortilla

Head Cheese

Screen Door

Fatty Corpuscle

Tungsten

Husk

HUMBERSCROTCH
FACTS

Stephen Hawking said: *How much wonder in a nebula, how much in the humberscrotch?*

In late 1800s, the humberscrotch was used as fishing lures in hopes to catch the spring-run Columbia River salmon.

What was once called Lake Oswego was originally called Humberscrotch Swamp.

Hall of Fame basketballer Bill Walton, who led the Portland Trailblazers to the 1977 NBA championship, would often exclaim: *Humberscrotcha!* after slam dunking opponents.

Humberscrotch is in the Fungi kingdom.

ORANGE FERGUS
BRAIN ROT

Seeing all with his long eyes and quick heart. He simply cannot lose. Palms open, sweating (knees weak). Damn does he have the hands! He was once known for consuming hot chips and laying. Or was it lying? But now, moist and thriving, he knows to stay in his own swimming lane.

MONSIGNOR
SACRED TRADITION

As I prayed, I drank from minibar bottles, hidden in the palms of my hand. I prayed a lot and was known for my devotion. Appearances matter, that's what church tells me.
— Aloysius Parker

Items that can be hidden in prayer hands:
Vape
Candy
12-foot long silk scarf
Crucifix
Ouroboros
Seahorse
Cheat notes

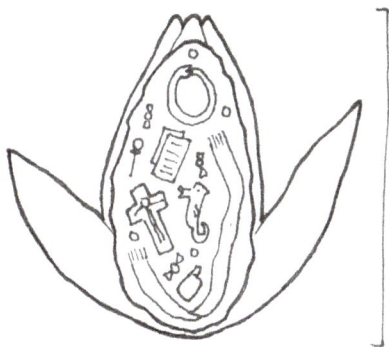

Alien
Candy

LIVERBLADE
PARABLE

She doesn't wear red for decades. He dreams in just purples.
The two of them get together, quit the color parable, mostly
cold turkey. Build the bitter little seed that got here now.
Here now. Now you know to give the basins, the organs.
Familiar with calcification, rain shadow. Absolving terrain as
it regenerates. Splits.

MISTER GARABALDI
SEASON 7

Christ, how many haven't known. The insane crystallite under gift, the dust of the fiction, upsetting. The stamen prey. The villain himself, that house of names. Iannelli. Riviera. Dimpled in oil. Focaccia song. Guimo. Edwin. DiSalvatore. Missus.
Why is the consonant? Expensing
Alveolar or rhotic? Early notables
A pendulum of migrations
Some of the settlers
Aboard the
Tarnish
Again
Came in laving
Arcadia spelled
The feline supinka
Ipomopsis Polyantha
Forgot the word that opened it, dimension, for decades:
Presto!

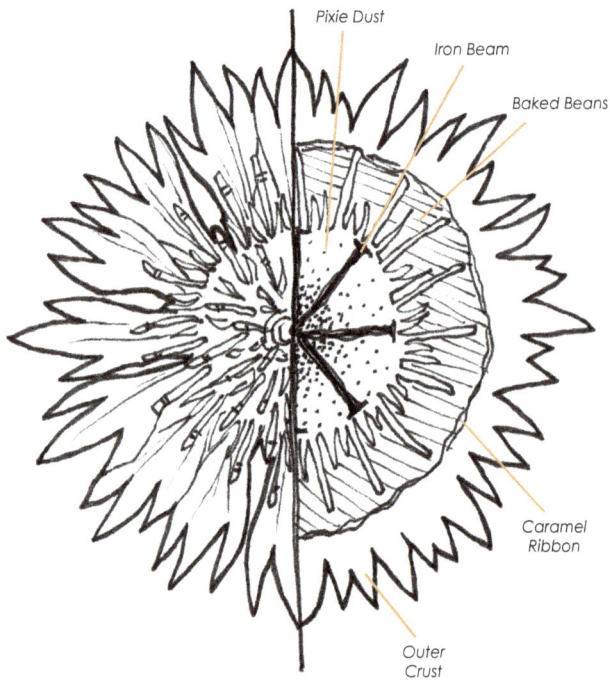

Pixie Dust

Iron Beam

Baked Beans

Caramel
Ribbon

Outer
Crust

WILLAMINA
INVESTIGATION

Got the cicadas on tape, caught more and more breeze, collected up their carapace. As far out. As tart bit, as amalgam. Granted identity at the cinderblock stage. To get up the beckon for it. Eventually the spiders and the heirs show. Everyone in chrysanthemum rock. Cut that way, a variant, way before. The slaughter comes up late. Their medley undone, especially carted around in sweaty fists. It sounds like canon, all raining flatter, all chamomile cake. As low as the spread gets. As late as the fog stays put. Lost count of the pastry layers, the scurried self. Put filberts, of course, via praline, cream, frangelico.

ORONGANADE
SPELL

1. Gather tools:
   paper
   glue
   petals
   star anise
   whole cloves
   shovel
   matches
2. Place dried petals in mortar
3. Add clove, star anise, intention
4. Crunch into fine powder with pestle
5. Draw ambitions in glue on paper
6. Sprinkle mixture atop
7. Burn and bury

Isn't something just lofted like that? And you couldn't have known to imagine it. Ignore stuff like peeling off the pear's sticker, and shatter glass confetti. Instead the mural and creeper vine up fourteen stories. The soundtrack you started, bridgeless. The nine-year-old author, maybe, but certainly that I'd entertain and have real flowers. Mirror or gallery. Long table. Writing a menu. You go on with the perpendicular prize, something in the doodle said it. That fulfills some sort of precipice, then the books start coming, dedicated script and sugar, you wouldn't be so secular. Protested outside the auditorium, that symbolic accessory. Stay mutating the line, as you, generations in, percentages. Differentiated. Return in a flume of triumph, up for the gentling, more.

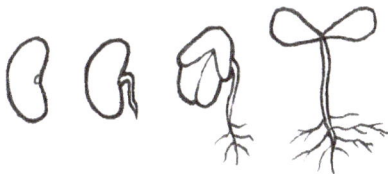

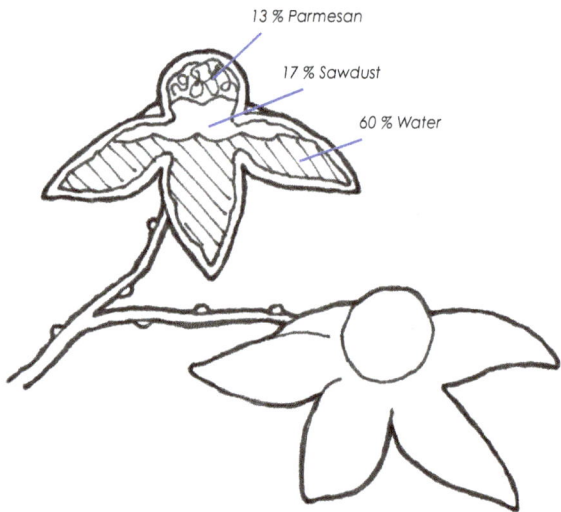

13 % Parmesan

17 % Sawdust

60 % Water

MURGATROYDS
SCIENCE FICTION

They are already here. I'm not sure how you haven't noticed. Bulbous and slick, growing as though they've been there all along. More intelligent than you or me. Murgatroyds are tuned in, they can survive anywhere. We can't do that. We can't survive. We are barely existing.

They pulse to communicate, connected through branches, stretching out and curling in, their petals 60% water, just like us. We can't hear them, but they're laughing at us.

FIBONACCI
SURVEY

How have you executed the sequence? How have you defined faithfulness? How much lava have you seen, expected? How does the second person make you feel? Do the blues ingest? Such an ancient flake came off the canvas, have you kept it? Pretended? Can you manage the makeshift signal? Overtamed the intuition, right? Where did you stash it at? The emphatic, spritzing series. Which version exudes you, ever-gladed? Which waver are you still stuck in? And not at all? Bringing around that special contagion. A lifelong binge of flavor, yes?

BINGUS
ACAPELLA

Bingus bangus bungus bongus bengus sometimes byngus.
Gather 'em up. Chant into a tin can. Music over open flame.
Hear the echoes multiply through the canyons.
A chorus down the river.
An ensemble into the ocean.

HYPNOSIS FOLDS
ALMANAC

The endowed come-up. Go asking for molecule, existential measure, again. Hold the synapse a new way for five hours. Then again. This here is a ceiling dolphin, a figurative buffalo, a porous starfish. That I'll make it back and split the winnings, bestow the great detail. The crepe need. An infamous crushing, amateurly. Put the wine stamp, the wrinkles all life long, came from a silky, tight pod. A hilarious little irresistible ditty unfurls. Giant moon of envy. Havers of. Some cling shrugged and thermal vents chugged, a trance hung, hate to be scolded, told what to do but: feel free to stay on the highest hypnotic rung.

Gabagool
Capsule

Barleycore

Harvest
Waltz

Yeast
Cousin

ANATHEMAS
SOLILOQUY

All this while the magnets demanded. While the crows came. Then, the doses get put in a spreadsheet. The collective sieve, pushing. It feels inflated, a second mash for the railing. Generational still. Botanical tank. Limoncello loyal. The grasshopper in the shuttlecock while it waits, the snake parachute. All unsalted butter and cankles and star-spangled banner and Hamilton and leafblower. Whatever rant, cruise ship buffet. Casual poison they don't tell you about. Discussing our fictional drugs. Could go a couple of ways, aloofly. All winter lambing. Alien in the cradle. Drinking from our finest treeline tarns. Caught it late and saw the many dream assemblies. Wrist kiss, depending. Let us know the echo starve. A sticky fridge. A wet sleeve, all over.

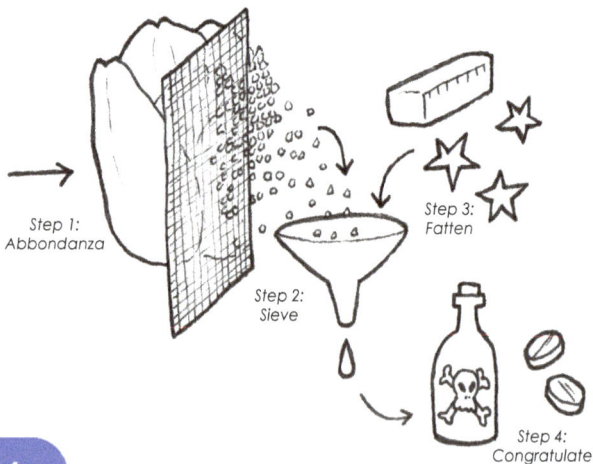

Step 1: Abbondanza

Step 2: Sieve

Step 3: Fatten

Step 4: Congratulate

NORMAN
ODE

Oh, precious prince.
Oh, ostentatious dandy.
Oh, undressed for all to see.
Oh, please.
Oh, delicate scholar.
Oh, sugar-coated.
Oh, unmistaken.
Oh, innocent I loved once.
Oh, empirical wonder.
Oh, ballad of soft touch.
Oh, what if.
Oh, chosen one.
Oh, artificial diplomacy.
Oh, pardon you.

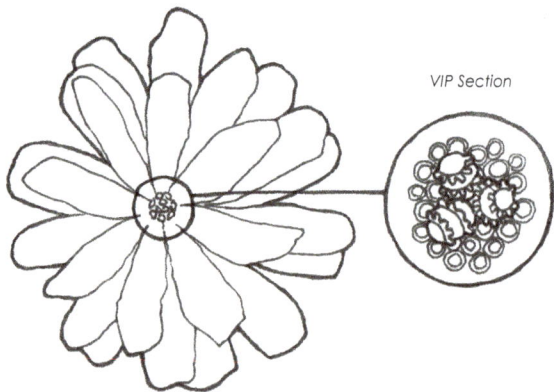

VIP Section

GIDDY LAMPLETS
ELEGY

There's nothing you can't say about the anemone. They globe good. They gladhand the September sidewalk, plush like you never knew, slicing up the portraits to send all over the midwest. They're coming toward the land of the window. The arrival you dread for, in all ways. Like chocolate-milk-matte shine, of course we want their waving ring, their soft appendages. Their leaves like royals. Put me onto the emerald name. Stop on our successive blocks, corners. No foil. No hinges. No one has to ask *whose* about the utopia. The stacks licked off like icing, the grape-berried preservation. Like how we have the vinegar capital, the mistlike fuzz from the center strung. Of the truest stuff. Of the late morning, along, its filled satellite, so very adoring.

FOXTROTTER
A GUIDING LIGHT

Laying under ten thousand blankets—suffocating, yet comforted by the weight. Body feeble and uneasy, sustained by oatmeal, coffee...otherwise detached. Distant. Despondent. Collapsed. Then, gathering pieces, refusing to let go. Poor thing should exercise? eat better? go outside? Poor thing was ambitious? a go-getter? a foxtrotter? Perhaps.

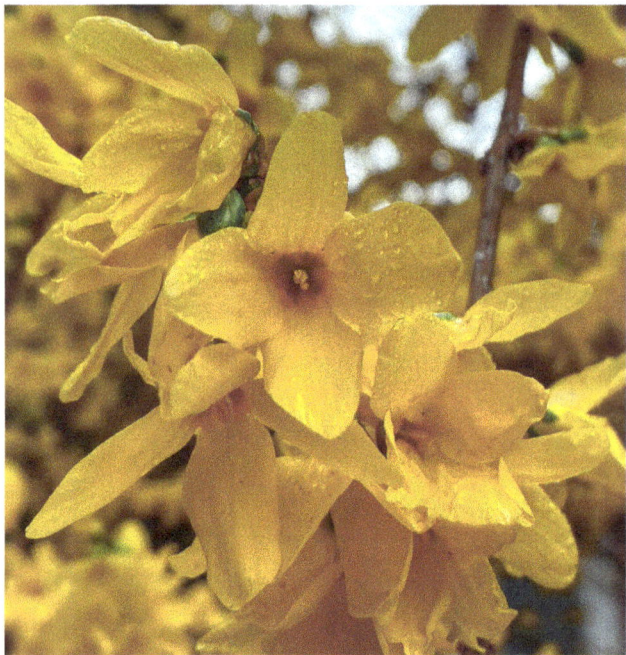

EAR MULLET
TRENDSETTING

The ever revered ear mullet. Looks good tousled and tossed, like that sad bagged salad in the back of your refrigerator you forgot about. But not rumpled! Never rippled. Appropriate for semi-formal, though some might say best for semi-truck. Seen here in "tequila sunrise," the ear mullet also comes in bronge, greige, vermellonion. Or perhaps a peppy puce & pewter polka dot?

SMEGIN BERSERS
FIELD ENTRY

Smegin Bersers primarily grow around community gardens in populated urban areas. Their pollen is spread by the Western Harbinger Bee which is most attracted to the flower's sour candy flavor and bubblegum aroma. These creatures spread pollen to nearby suburbs, infecting container gardens, and pitting heterosexual couples against each other as they slowly go mad from the infectious scent.

Paradoxically, they have the opposite effect on hummingbirds, whom, once infected, build nests together and grow old in total monogamy.

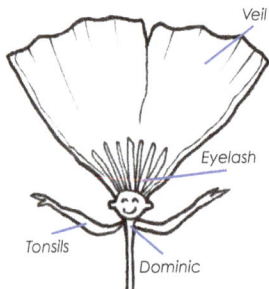

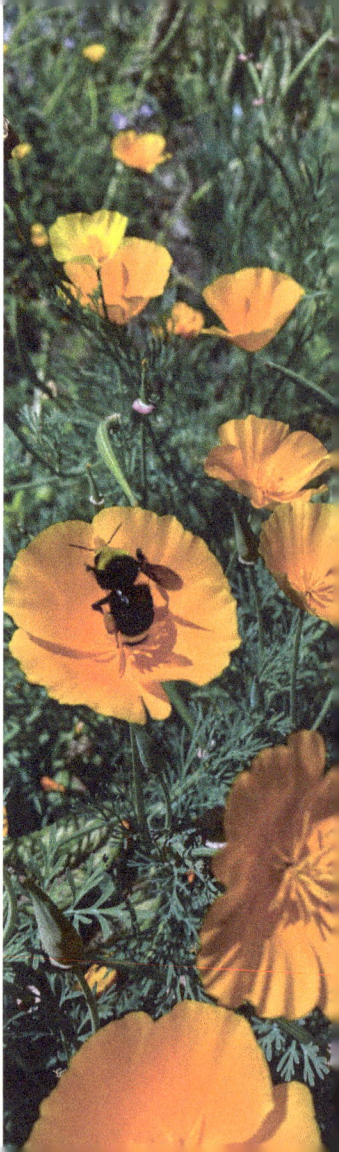

Veil

Eyelash

Tonsils

Dominic

Every sort of strong endeavor. There is no uphill here, or indistinguishable tones of brown and gray. No, it's never that faithful, the nearly-year-round bloom. Making moss beds and bouncing through. The sentences petaled, kept up the vitamin appetite, the coaching into a specimen. The bars of that fatuous manner. Spots that trademark the leaves, roundabouts with the best bushes, cedar shelter cover effacing the relatively young pavement. Get under, go on. Vault louder, kitchen counter makeout, letting the sulfites swarm. Our attention branches, gathers. Get off the simulation and see the leaves waving, go in for a sniff already. Amen.

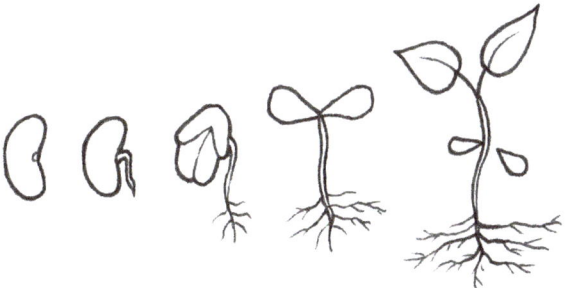

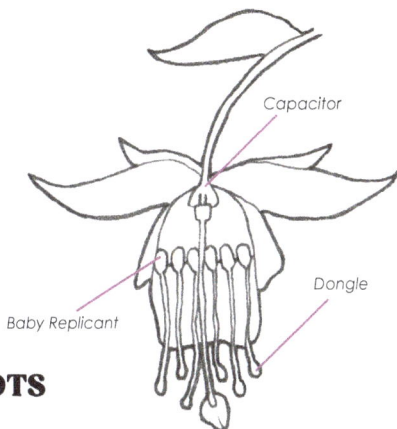

Capacitor

Dongle

Baby Replicant

JUNDLE PLOTS
EULOGY

Remembered best for the time they took their teeth out and sang hakuna matata, drunk at the annual Superbowl party. They always brought the fun and they always ended up sleeping it off on the couch before my mom let them drive home. [Pause for laughs.]

They were born in 1976, conceived at the end of the Vietnam War to a father who had PTSD and a mother who had never left her small Midwest town. They are survived by their younger sibling, who promptly moved to Thailand at 18 and sometimes updates us via Facebook. They could not make it home for the service. They are also survived by their son who is currently stationed in Afghanistan because they wanted to make their grandfather proud and frankly didn't have the grades to do much else after high school. They also could not make it home for the service.

As my godparent, they were always there for me when I needed someone to talk to. They snuck me alcohol at family functions, and took me to my first baseball game. I will always remember them fondly.

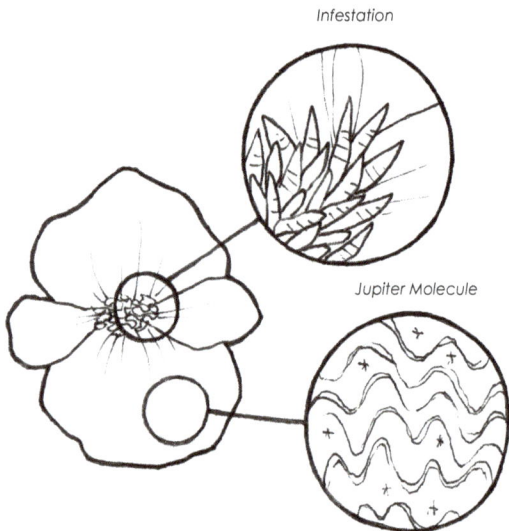

Infestation

Jupiter Molecule

COMPOUND BERRY
FRUIT INDEX

Back to pulp. If you're doing consistent fire. We keep agreeing on accident. The language isn't. Out draping, ponytail, mid-pink. Up to the cold waist, to the flexed collection. Later states, the swords of pineapple. The shape supreme. Searching the orchid archive. For an early velveteen prototype. A parenchyma conglomerate. You glimmer into the birthplace. Shouldn't hurry, making blaze. Joyous nerves for once, their candy balletic, chaos-raised. Like the lock expects it, fiddly. A shine you look after, result from. A desirable oblong sweep. Contemplate the paste, the compound berry, back at it.

WATERLOO
INVENTION

The spice divides on your palate. You pull up for the prickles. The regional drug. The mistaken poison dispelled, simmered out. The structure you left there, the page stood so still and the icons revolved on it. Holding her in the atrium, dipping over the gleaming banister, never been so kissed. Filling thistle for the lattice. So hard to mustard, violet it all away. Watering indefinitely. Betting by the ordained coils, sarcocarp. A non-newtonian player, east coast ponies, memorized. Really any likelihood. Also, luck.

SHORTHAND MEREDITHS
RECIPE

No one calls it longhand anymore. How much can you access the old swords, at all, the pills in their hiding place. The storm catalogue gets fancier. Absolution sweating out. The dainty tricks, the lizard spit out, twinned floating, mid-lake. Pre-bee pollination. Shorthand Merediths, dripping. A sleep that stretches itself, root-like, a vital accident, cookie from the flowers, universal tonic.

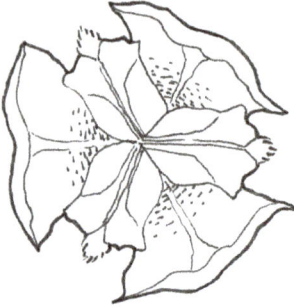

Godless Variant

Burning Swirl

Hairless Pineapple

TRAPTEZE
HOW-TO

1. Advance
2. Seize and straighten
3. Lift overhead
4. Broaden at the edges
5. Turn outward
6. Applaud
7. Return to converge
8. Look up and implore
9. Lock the nexus
10. Rotate down the back
11. Open fingers wide
12. Inflate the fixture

SUPER GHEE
NATURAL MEDICINE

Mush berries before yellows blossom. Apply to eyelids for better sight and improved cognition, promoting little to no sleep. Side effects may include discoloration of pupils and expansion of irises until the whites are completely gone. Warning: you may not like what you come to see, or understand.

SOAP SCALLOPS
ANECDOTE

For every small child's mouth, *fuck* is the most delicious. *Fuck*, I used to scream, running to the bathroom door, the only with a lock. The soap my mother had put in my mouth was not natural. It must have been Dawn or Dove, something strong and permanent, decadent as a scallop dinner.

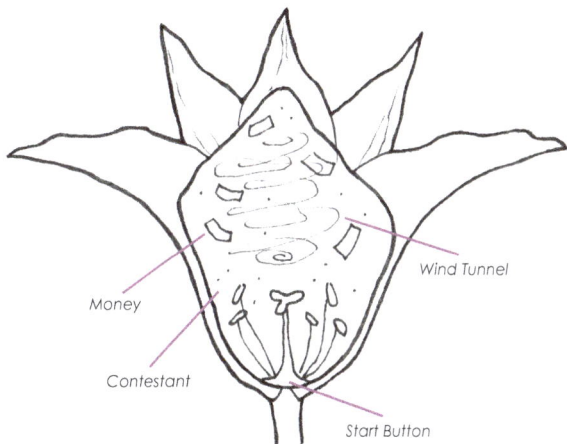

Money

Wind Tunnel

Contestant

Start Button

HUBBA BUCKS
HISTORY: PORTLAND

A member of the monocot family, Hubba Bucks were a prized fashion item in late 1800s Portland, either pinned to the lapel of a gentleman's coat or presented as a corsage's centerpiece for cotillion debutantes.

Although the plant is not edible, revered culinary expert James Beard (who was born and raised in Portland) claimed that Hubba Bucks are a perfect companion plant to onions: *Mother used to plant Hubbas with the onions; and I don't think I have tasted a more robust bulb anywhere since. Even from Les Halles. I told this to Julia Child, and she said the French plant, a similar monocot, called Les Bouquins, accompanied their shallots.*

A group of Hubba Bucks is called a conglomerate.

FRECKLES
SERENADE

Prequel to Limberlost, century turn, the swamp fiddle praying. Could read about the custards forever. Full full tick. The prophetic pretty toxin. You give the beauty hunt. Living in any antidote. Talk to the pupae, the bulbs. That you're being thought about. Such a stack. As dewy as it gets. Remember to align with the questions more. Have them explain themselves. If this time stalls, if this gauzed bell was less beautiful. We successfully ignored the alkaloids. Making the May laps. Pull the coastal ditch. Loyal high. Spouting out their conspicuous lack, squealing, like site seven, the slick sleeping bag across the grass. The liver worry, peverada, lobe, tongue. Oh medicinal crook of pharmakon (where you are on the swoop.) Find our domestic copies if you never had the bass. We just have the pity creek. The newly infected estuary. Got to grow it out and dug all by myself. Fresh chromosomes. Could really flex, some jewels in the cargo. Could be. This is how the crinkle smooths. The myth hangs on for much longer. Flares through. Are you gave into, pulled over, harvesting, side of the road palace.

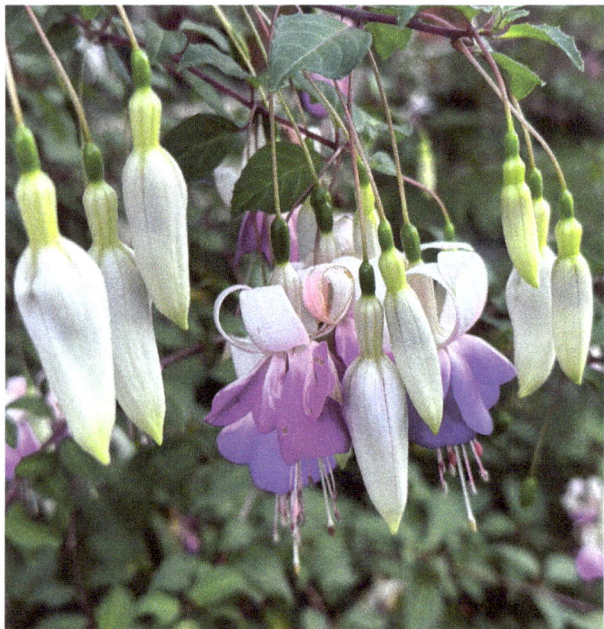

PEEPERS
WISDOM

We sweat droplets in summer like grape juice down a child's cheek, stain skin for luck, teach teenagers to dream big. Question everything. Think critically. Our petals emit wonder. Only the brave can be curious.

CELLOPHANE
A CRY FOR HELP

Or, a blue bordello without its wings...humbled? Unassuming?
A marvel without being ostentatious, available to admire if
you only took the time to notice.

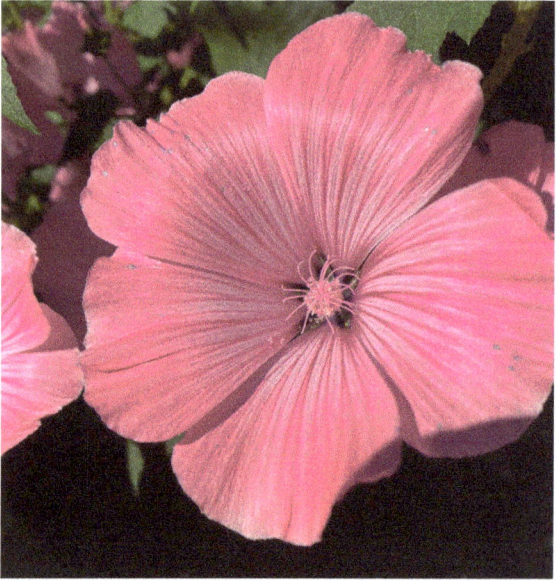

FLIM FLAMS
SEQUEL

Are the pish-posh of the mish-mash and all they talk about is flotsam. Jet some, kimono diplomat's son, and gibbous riptide. Then: fortuitous hotbox. Stay hy-phen for the rest. The desert hive relations. The mountain and any cash traces. The last phase of a Saturday, campus basement. The promise ring left copper stain and rolled right over to him, landed between. Upstairs counter-contra. Our natural compound. And we tried vampires, unsentimental. Grew on eachother. Towel rolled up in the gap between door and floor. Shower on, fountain of steam, kicking out the silly thirst, and that level of laugh.

SCANDALS
FABLE

You have vision, turning, catalpa-like.
With fuzz and vein (again) spearhead.
Expense the curve, the concentric
raw. Glicading in august. The famous
summers, vaselined. Fainted as some
come saddle. A trillion-year-red. A
century shaper, come up with dread,
hallways, and stadiums. The rescue
goes over to shape, tar bubbles and
numberless, embracing. The tree stars
left. Early on expected, came down
with fate. Nothing you can do. More
than one source, of course, so pet the
puckered cloth, the stacked jagged.
The scandalized mansion, we invent it,
let the revel forever, streakless. Water up
the beams, we're sloshing, outside of a
tradition, come on in.

Vaseline Alley

Tender Buckets

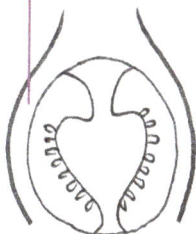

Moonchoke

Light Cruisers

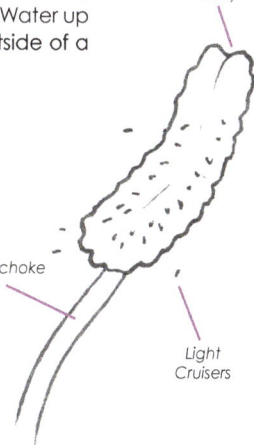

TUFF TUFFS
ETIQUETTE

Check your phosphorus, the yellow laying. The angles limbs come at. The dwelling special. Angelic clouds like that, sending them off. With plenty of disco. Creaturely amniotic, no adjective. The Gemini rappers, attenuated. The desk must be at a wall. High up canyoning, smoke through screen window. Dancepack through doorway. Offer up glassy, rolling-paper chalice, ten-dollar crémant. Even the corner store was fancy, the columns unimagined. The Hubbard street caves, you can't believe them, chain-link rave, everyone. Exhaust all in the spotlight, the customary spread. Between train and freeway, rack of takeover, filthying, of dance.

FANFARE
SPEECH

It assembles itself, biome oven, setting a cascade tube. The glare just before the tunnel. The moss home, tunnel again. Only at the orange does it close. Stay bundled, omnipresent, triumphing out in a taper. A sideways fill. An invisible prophecy that's covered in lichen. It's your turn to field the sample. How dare they call it libertine, the sentimental parking lot on the way in. The performance of a lifetime in the parking garage. The bootleg new era. Back when the town was analog, untangled by soffits, sable. An occasional lobby or porch, largely different temperatures of water. Fireworks twice. Gone off.

1. Creak

2. Double Punisher

3. Meloneer

4. Crest

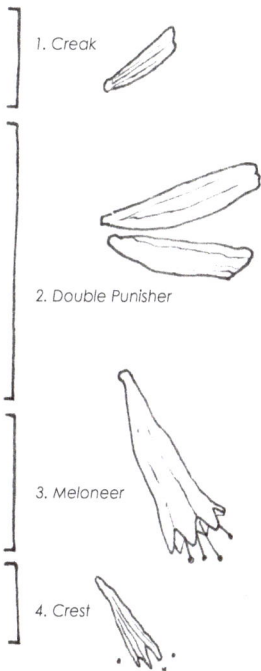

FANFARE LIFE CYCLE:
Creak to Crest

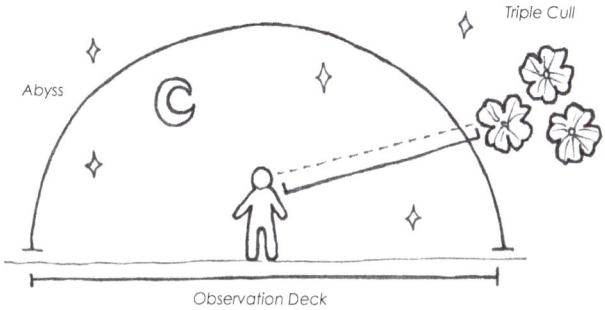

Triple Cull

Abyss

Observation Deck

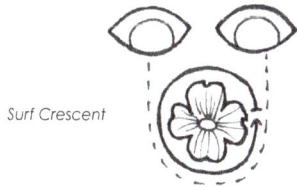

Surf Crescent

CATWOOD
EROTICA

The attraction is subterranean, frilling between the fascia. How do they know and will they be generous in offering to us? Almost never. Attach a light to the neck, maybe a camera, roam free overnight. In accordance with the size of the sky, track the diameter of vision; your affection irrelevant now. Larger animals scale with ease. You remain the voyeur you always were.

AFTERWORD

Howdy, Hyacinth. Godetia. Quince. Hellebore. Boundary. Sedge. Magnanimous magnolia, Coleoptera-made. Cornus florida. Sequoia. Mimosa. Madrone. Discretionary hedge. May pull. Biome. Mahonia aquifolium. Aster. Holy-like foliage. Back-to-back glories. Purple Sanicle. Deeply lobed. Zin e uh. Spreading Phlox. Streambank lupine. Rose of Sharon. Salal. Hoya. Allium. Discreet harvest. Currant. Column bine. Pacific bleeding heart. Coast Silktassel. Nootka. Thimbleberry. Vine. Trillium. Trusty chlorophyll. Raununclus. Garden party. Bog orchid. Mallow. All-over geranium. Digitalus. Dicentra. Mock orange. Sore ell. Sit cah. Showy Milkweed. Made velvety. Shade tolerant. Yare oh. Steam vie let. Hexandra. Latifolia. Starflower, for real. Piggyback. Roadside forsythia. Republic of petals. Thanks for the woodland, lace shapes, chocolate lily. We try to be perennial. Shade tolerant too. Stone crop. Yew. Fringe cap. Evergreen appreciation. Soil slippers. Solanum. Barbed goatgrass. Bohemian knotweed. Bull thistle. Spiny cocklebur, Cinquefoil. Briar. Datura. Buffalobur. Biddy-biddu. Syrian bean-caper. Camelthorn. Common bugloss. Crupina vulgaris. Cutleaf teasel. Toadflax. Dodder. Dog rose. Dyer's Woad. Brome. Garlic mustard. Hogweed. Yellow loostrife. Gorse. Halogten. Herb Robert. Campion. Direct our fondling wake their way. Say something encouraging. Hoary Alyssum. Leafy spurge. Jubata. Lesser celandine. Oblong. Clematis. Paterson's curse. Peavine. Pheasant's eye. Plumeless. Pepperweed. Puncturevine. Hemlock. Tansy. Taurian. Mugwort. Regards. Altissima. Welted. Bryonia. Archangel. Gomphrena globoso. Miner's lettuce. See you around town.

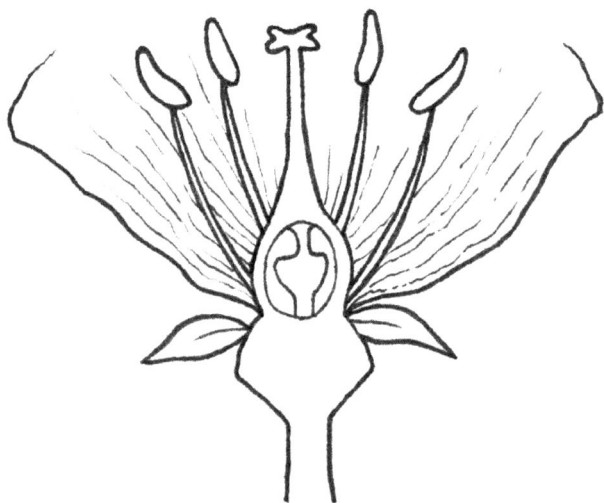

CONTRIBUTORS

KRIS COREY came up with prickly pear, fruit and flower. Curfewless, as much yellow, and agave. Even when the eyes well, admire with scratchy throat. Meet me at the corner garden. We'll walk there.

EMMI GREER was born and remains a flower disciple. Raised on purple alpine–rocky mountain penstemon and columbine. Now, floating around rose city, smelling every one into sneezes. Ask them about some of the best bushes in town.

EDY GUY acts in echopraxia. A flower in her hat, a flower in her palm, a flower in her defiance. She is made of great feeling resulting from the senses. For this, she thanks the flora.

RICH PERIN is a firefly. Twilight work. Or Apis melifera, here for the shaggy harvest. Blinking over the blooming ditch, all in the neighborhood glades. Go chthonic quince. Check out that saxifrage. Fuckers.

ELLEN ROBINETTE may or may not be known to steal flowers from around neighborhoods, but she promises that if she ever did, she only takes a few and leaves behind plenty for others to enjoy.

FIELD NOTES

FIELD NOTES

FIELD NOTES